Mandala : Love Art Vol.2
Coloring For Relaxation

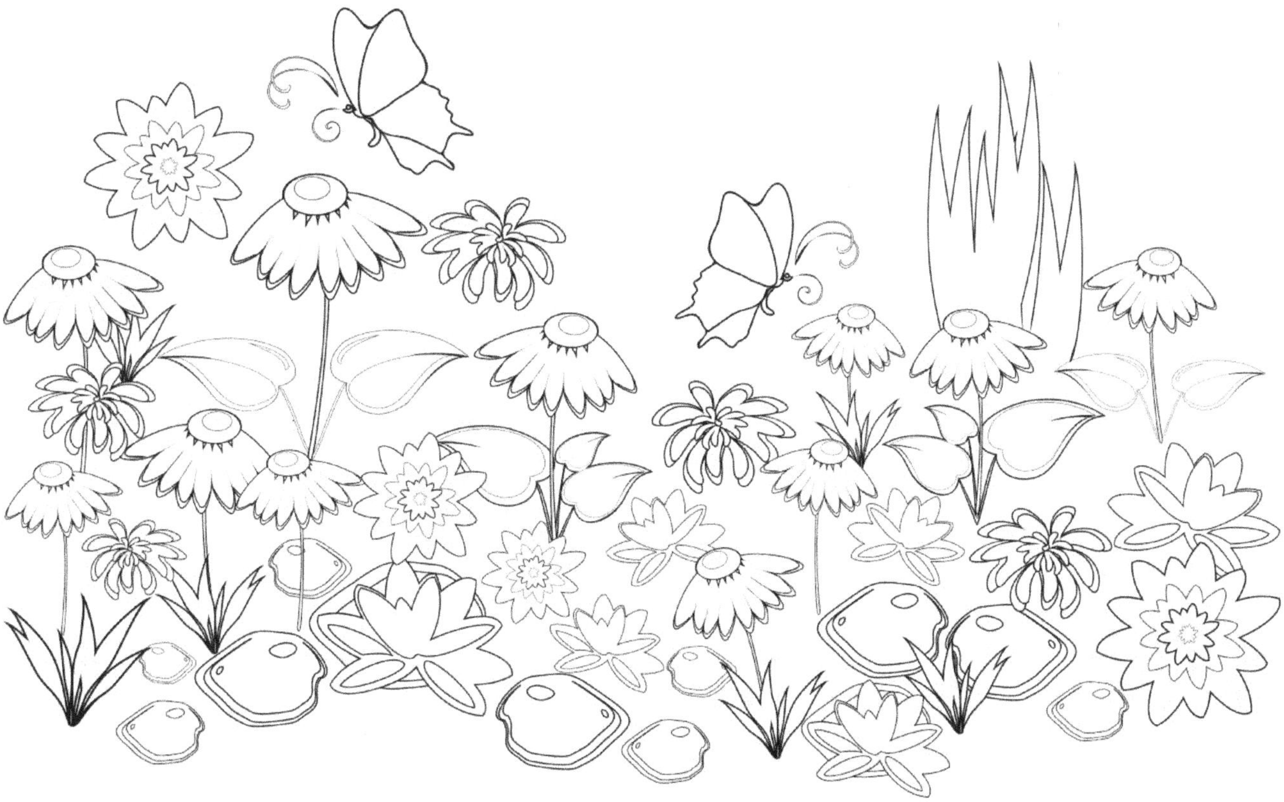

Sandra Hoffman

Mandala : Love Art Vol.2
Coloring For Relaxation

Copyright: Published in the United States by Sandra Hoffman
Published January 2016

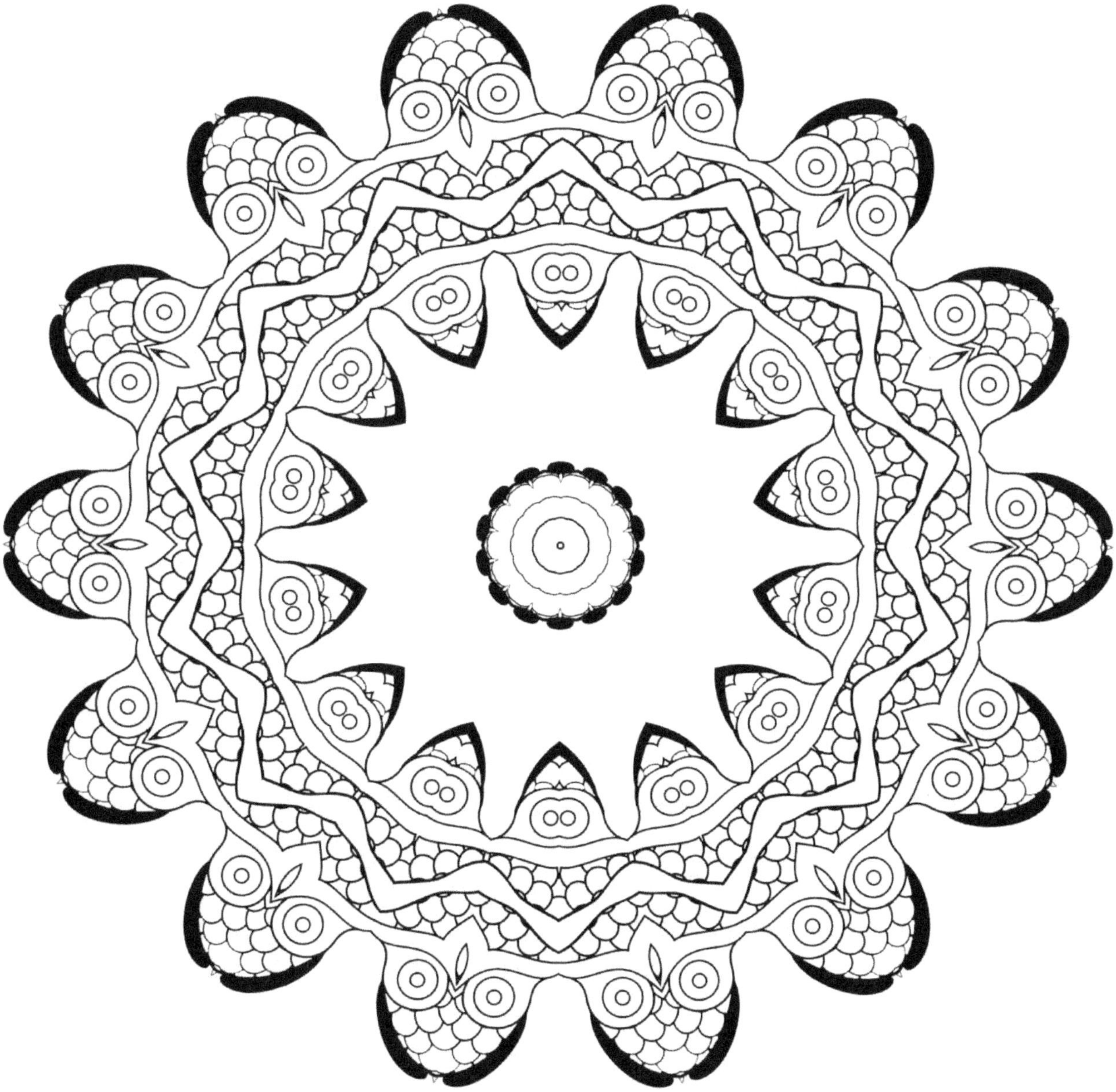

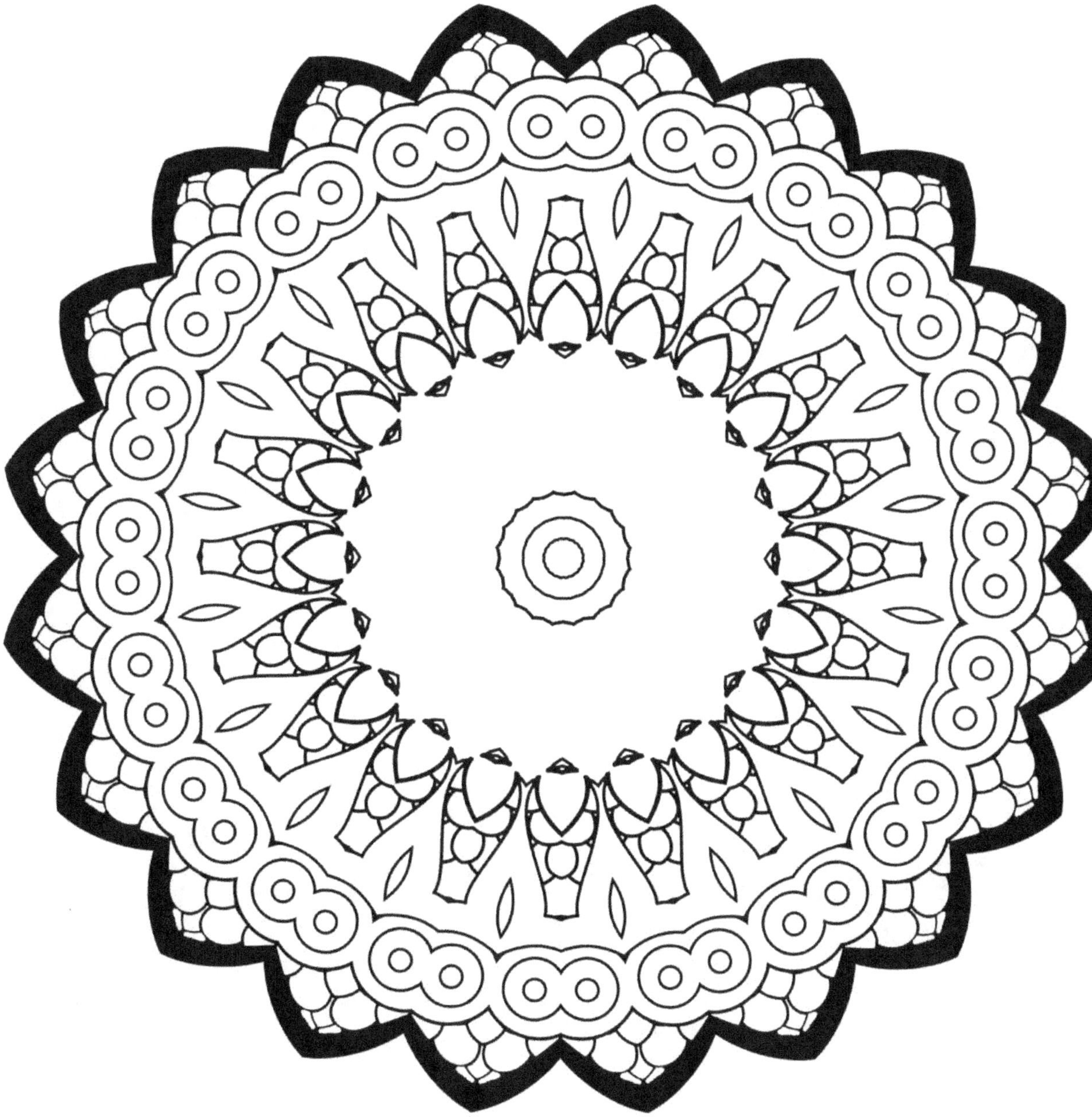

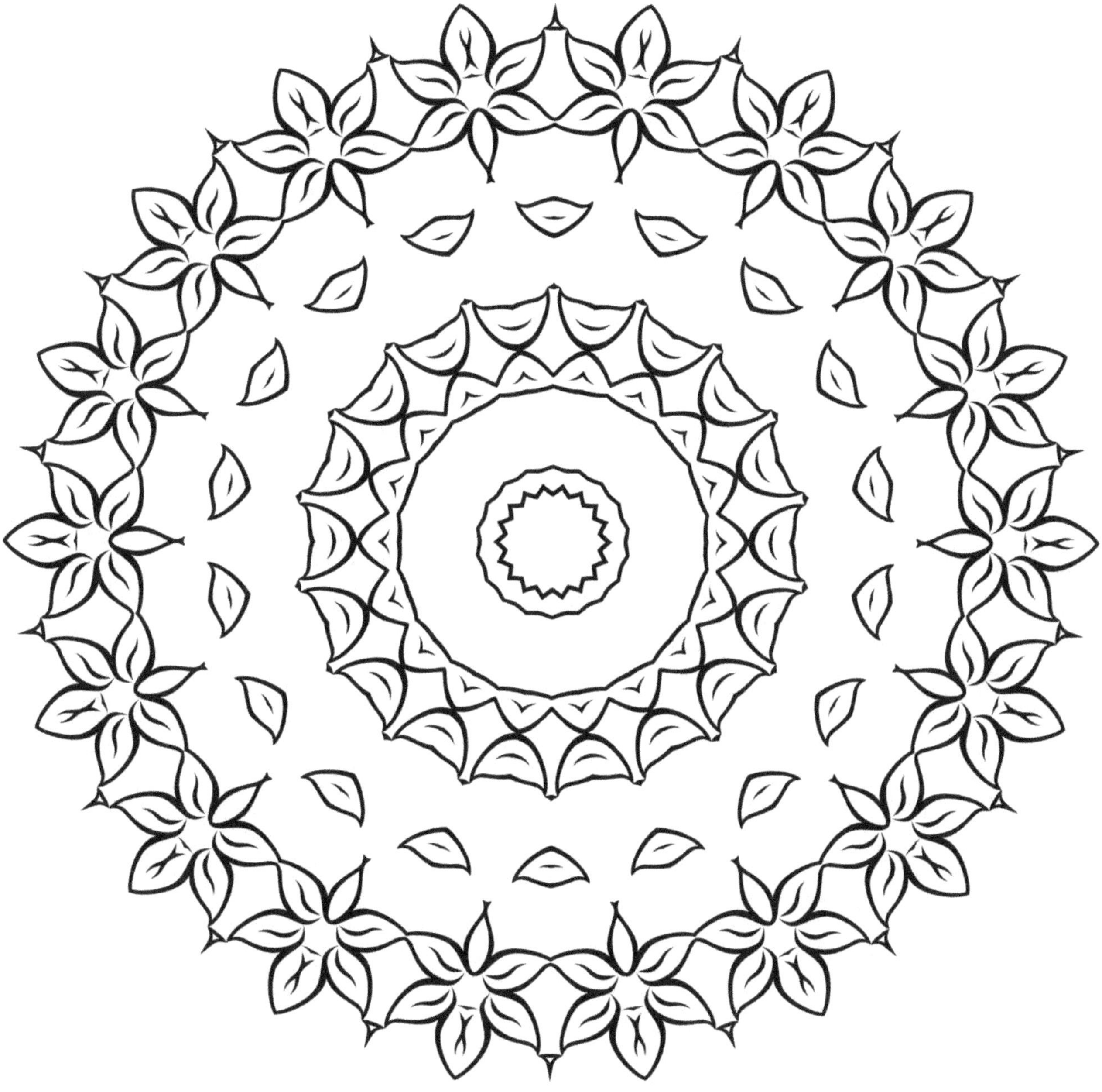

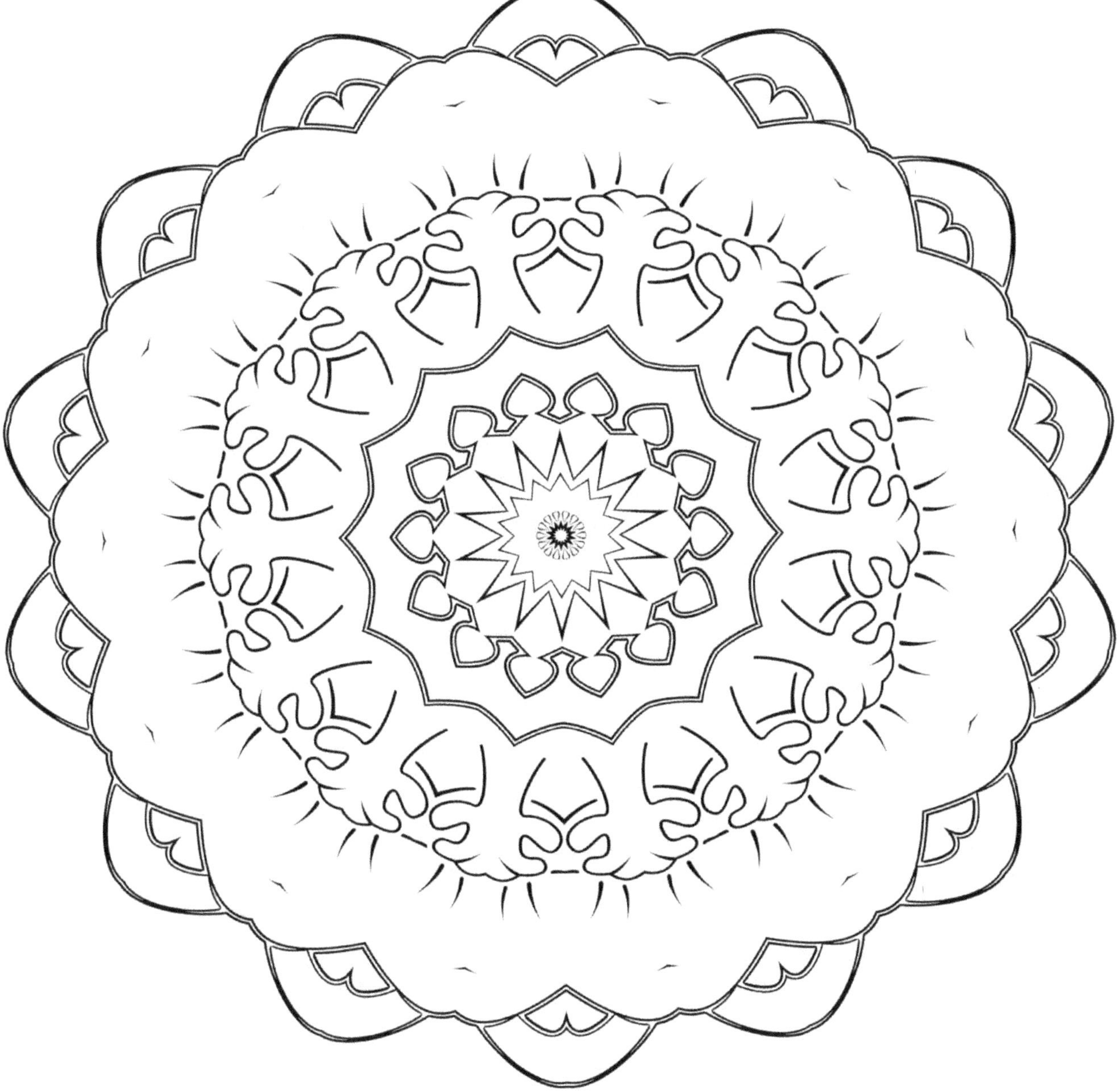

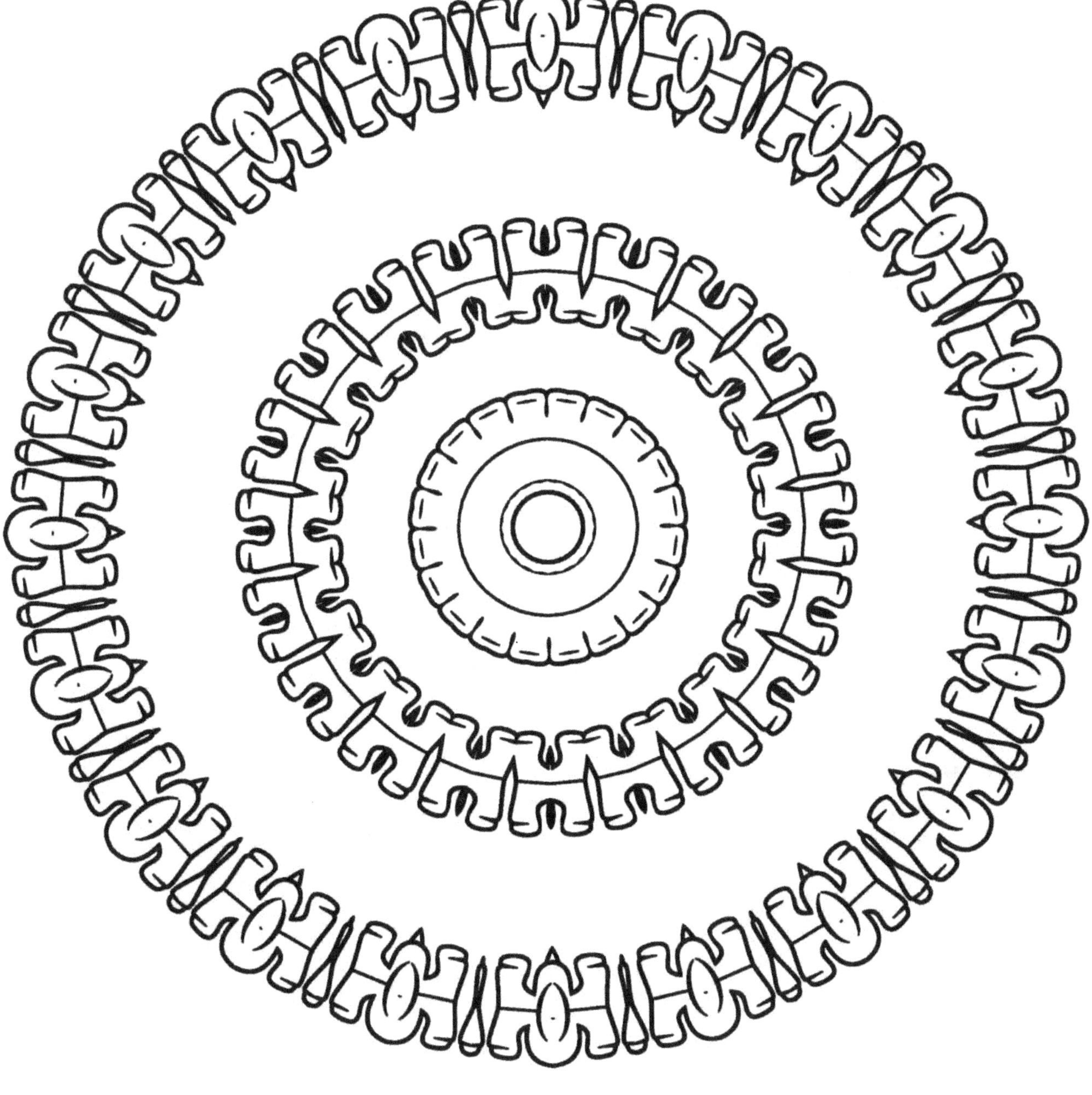

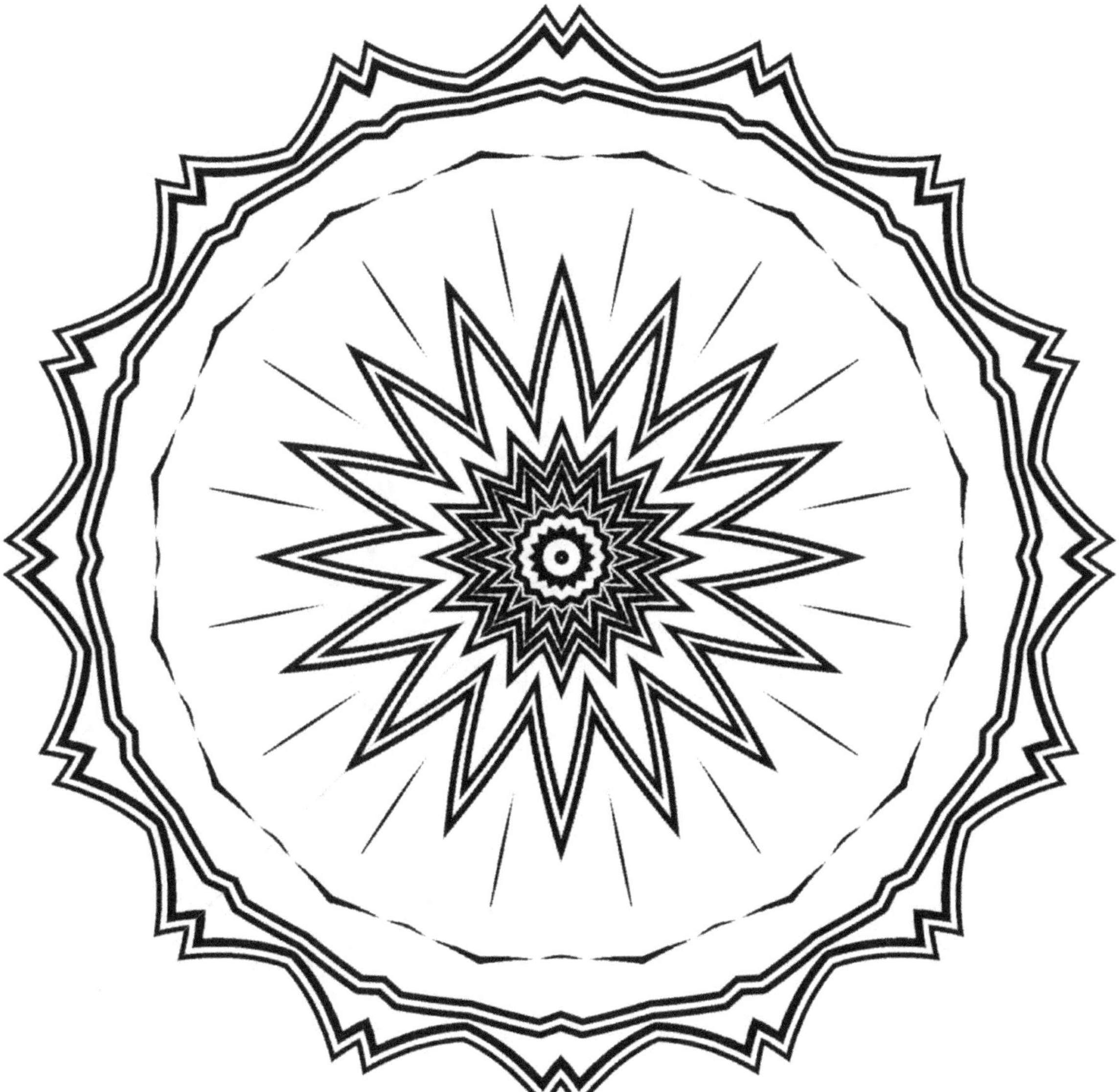

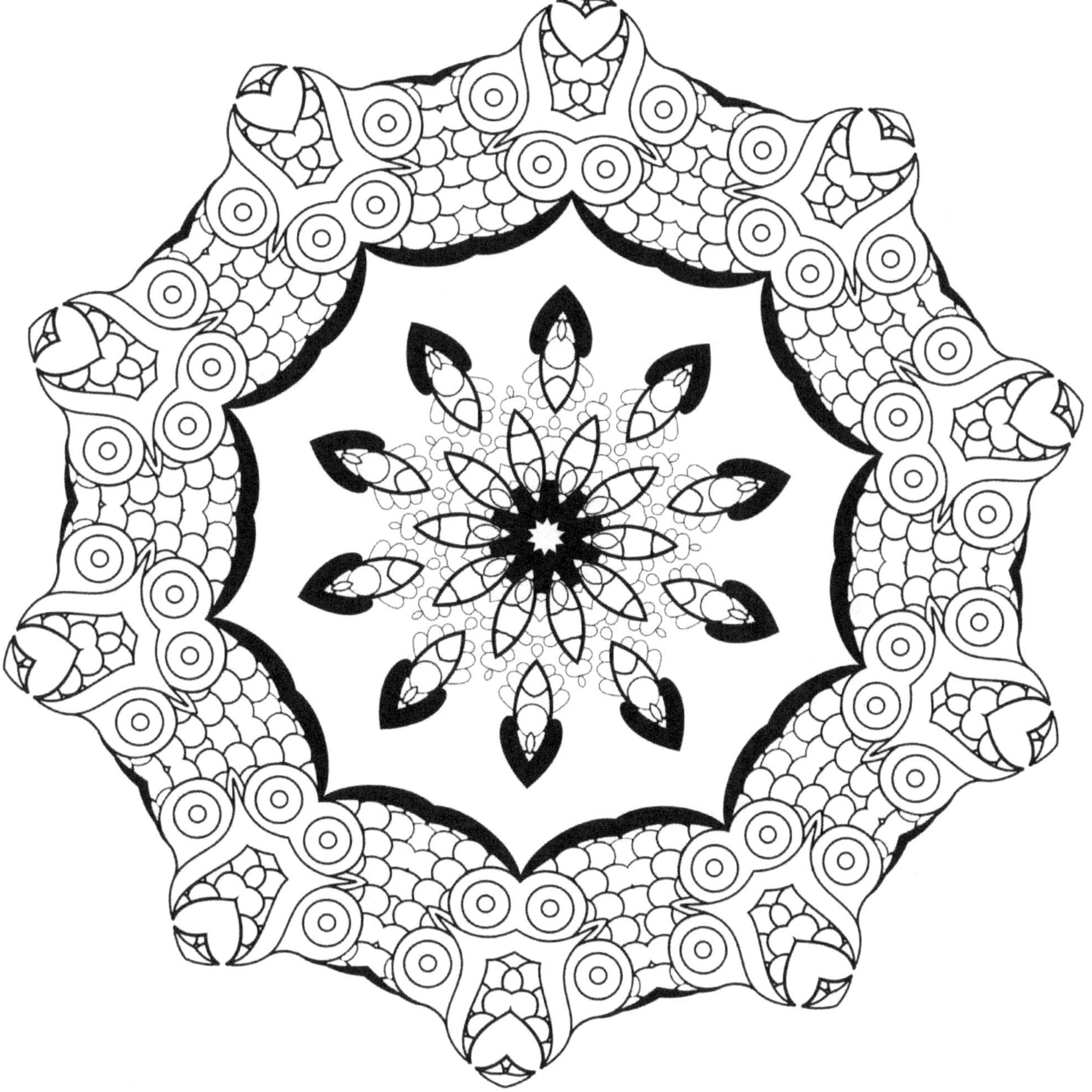

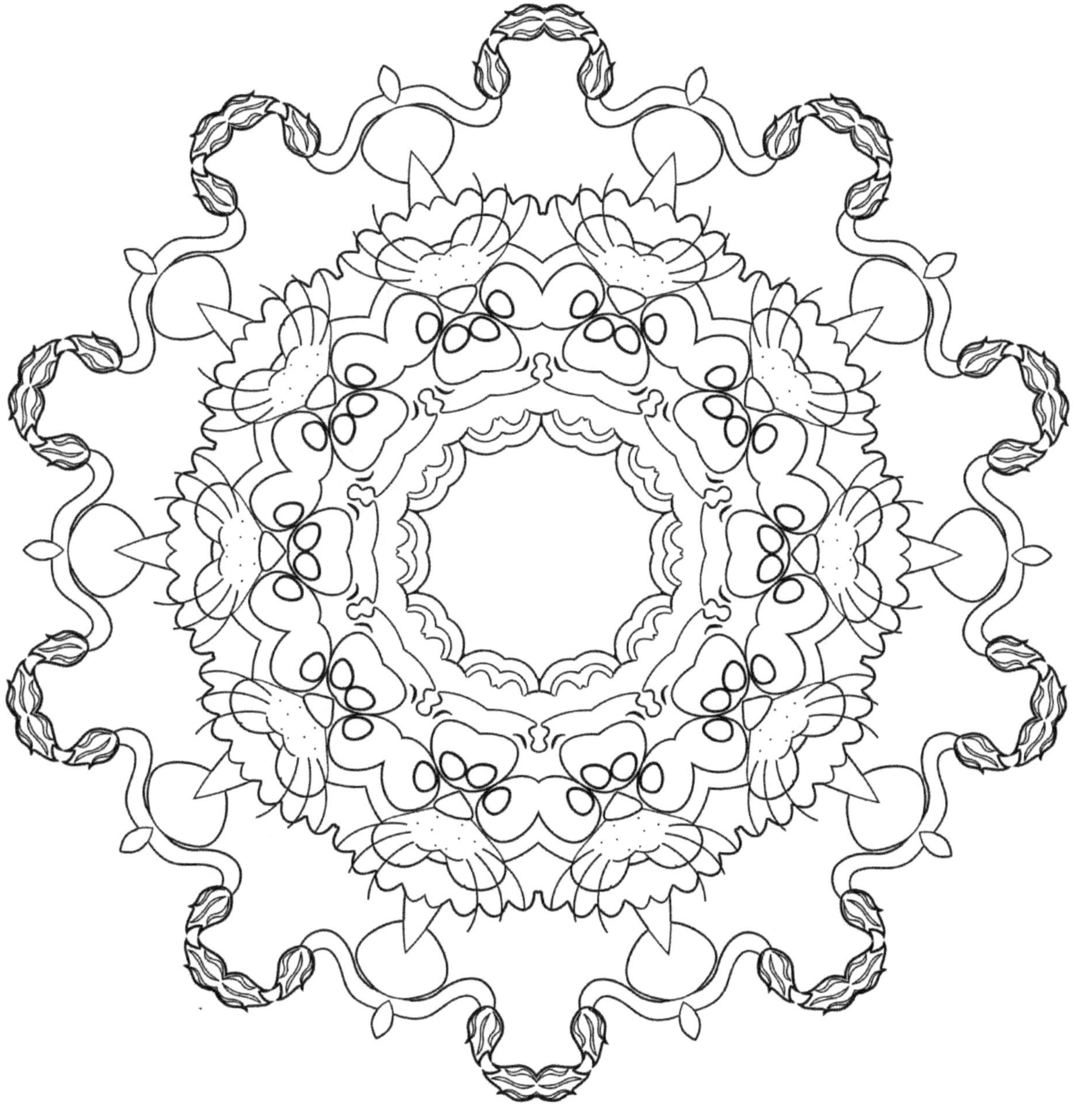

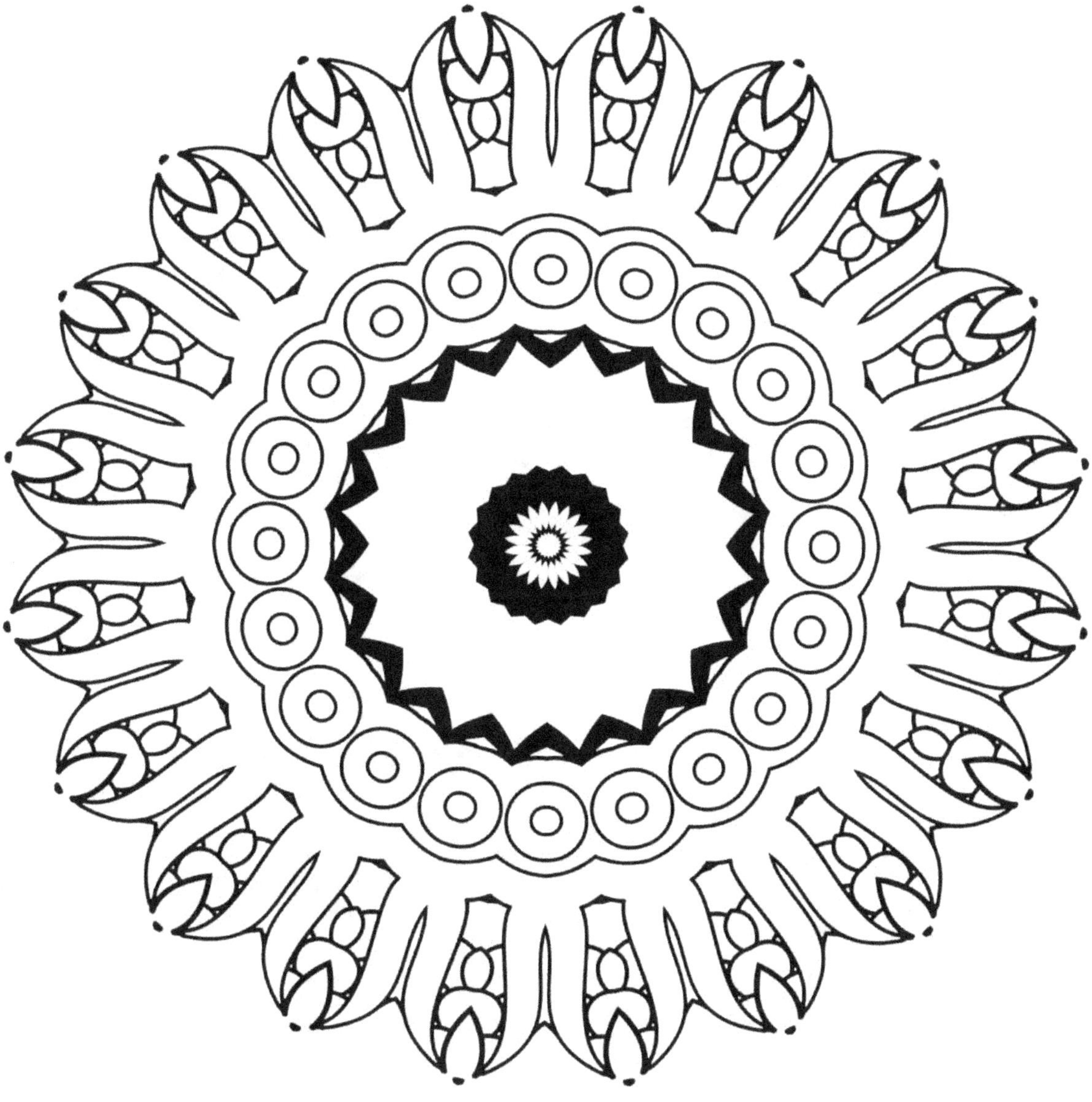

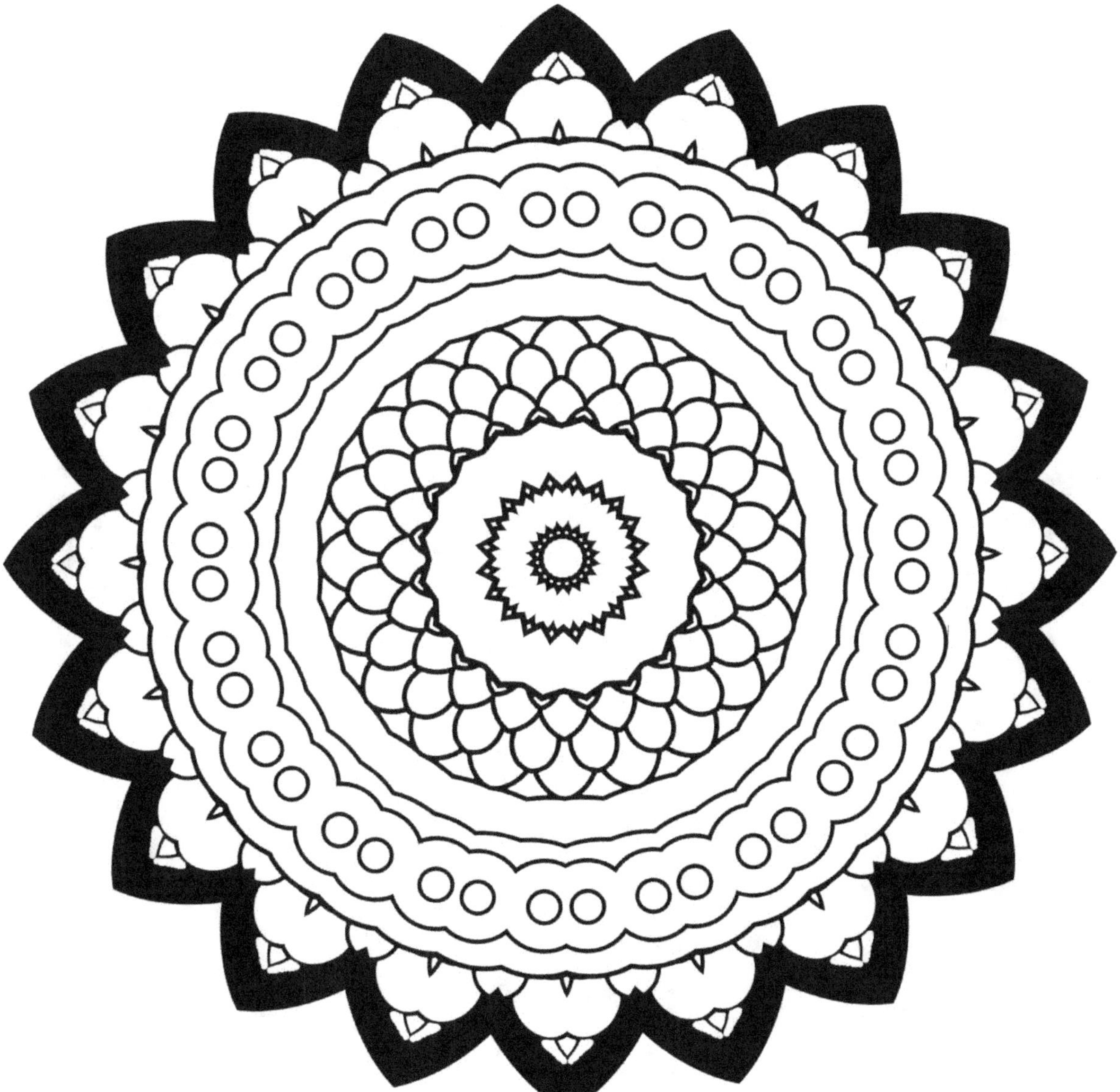

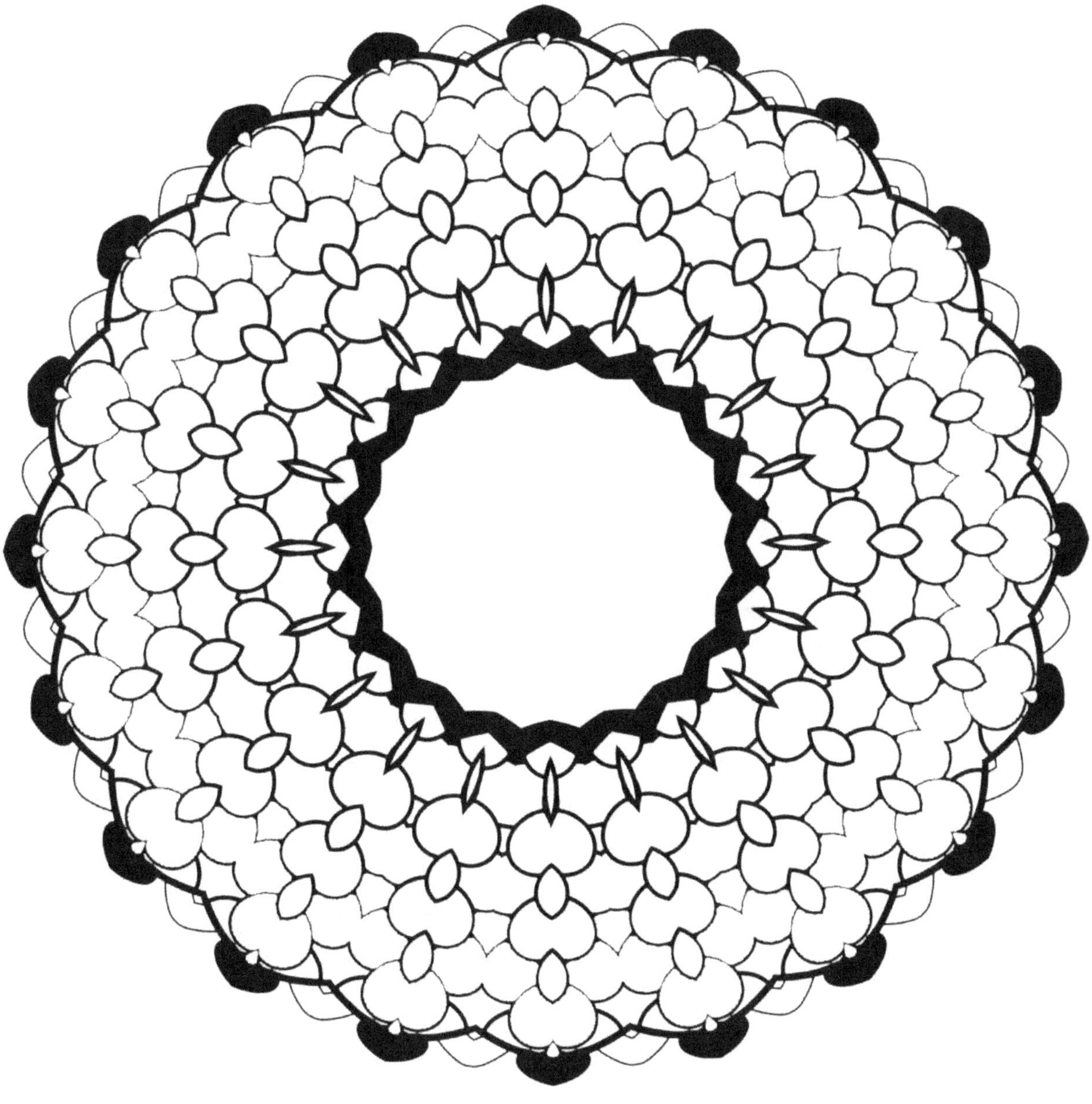

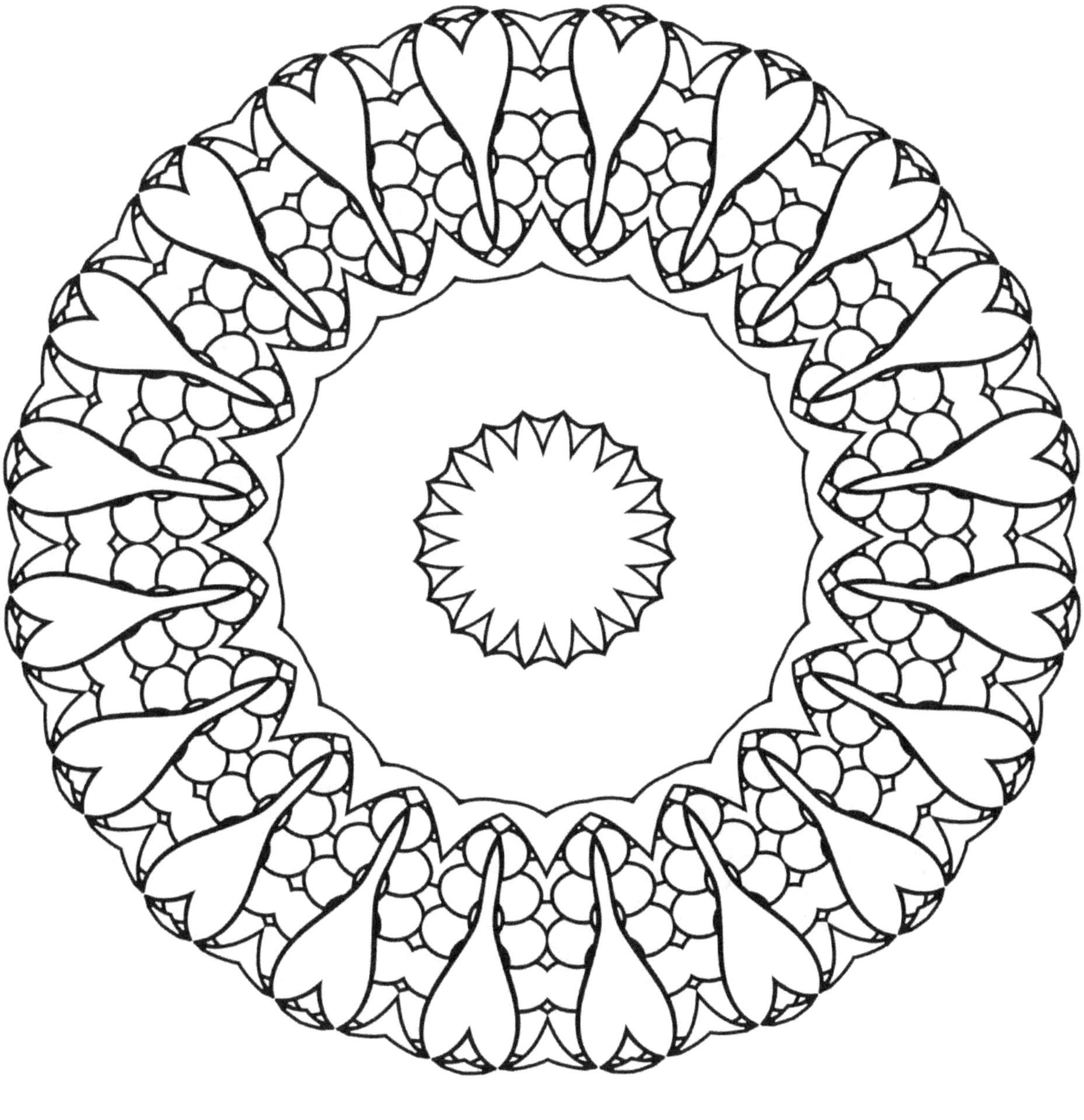

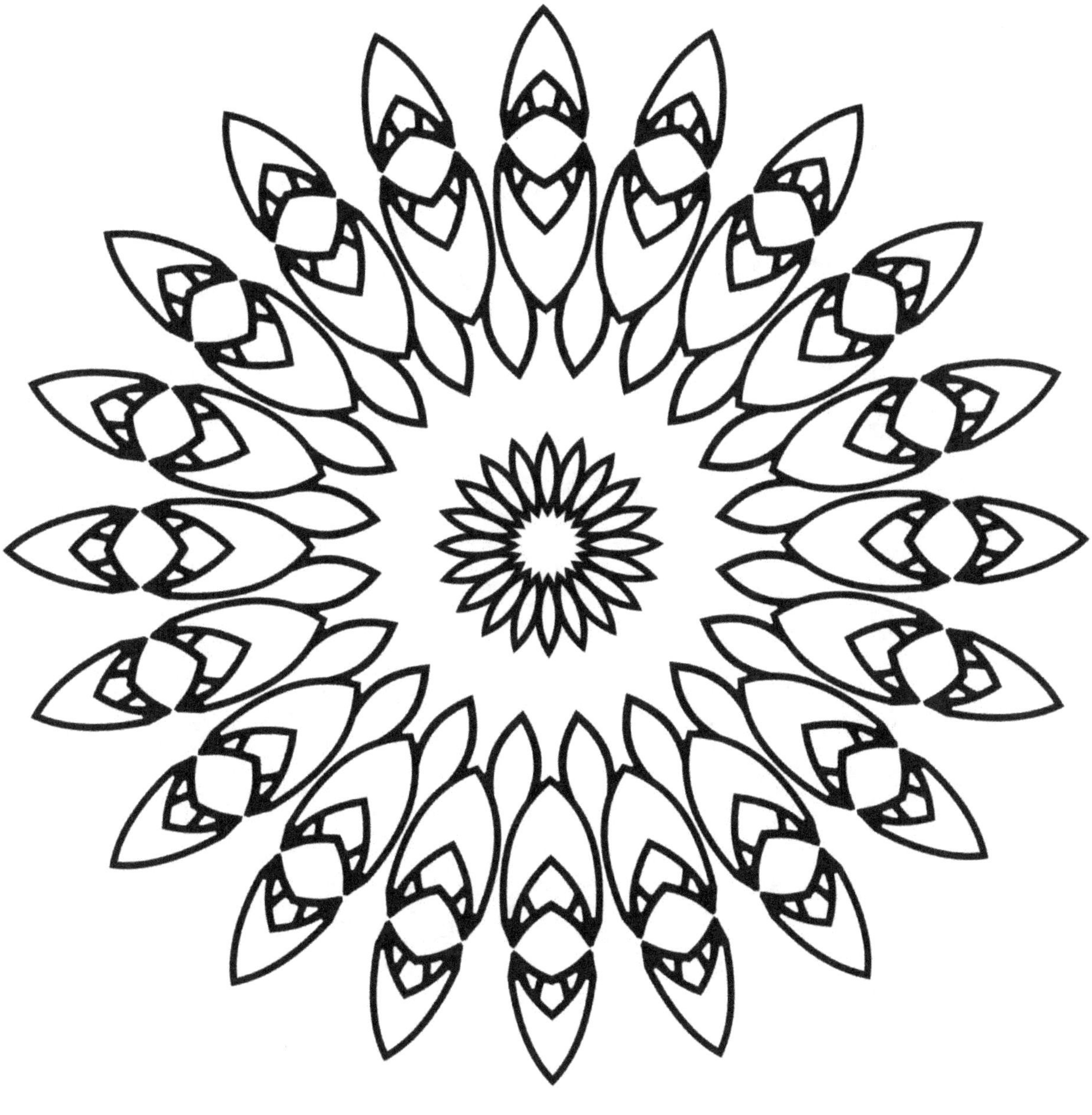

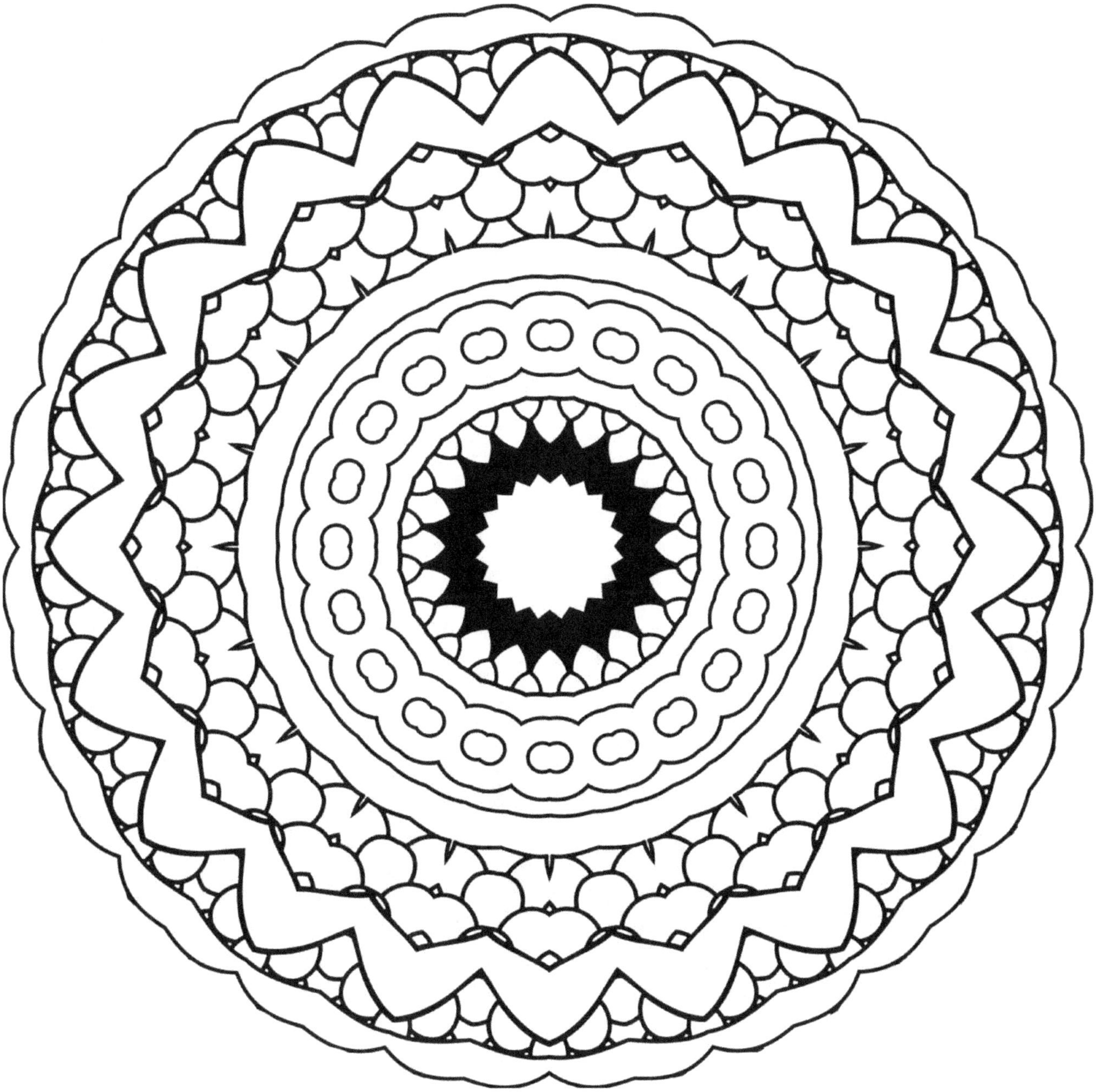

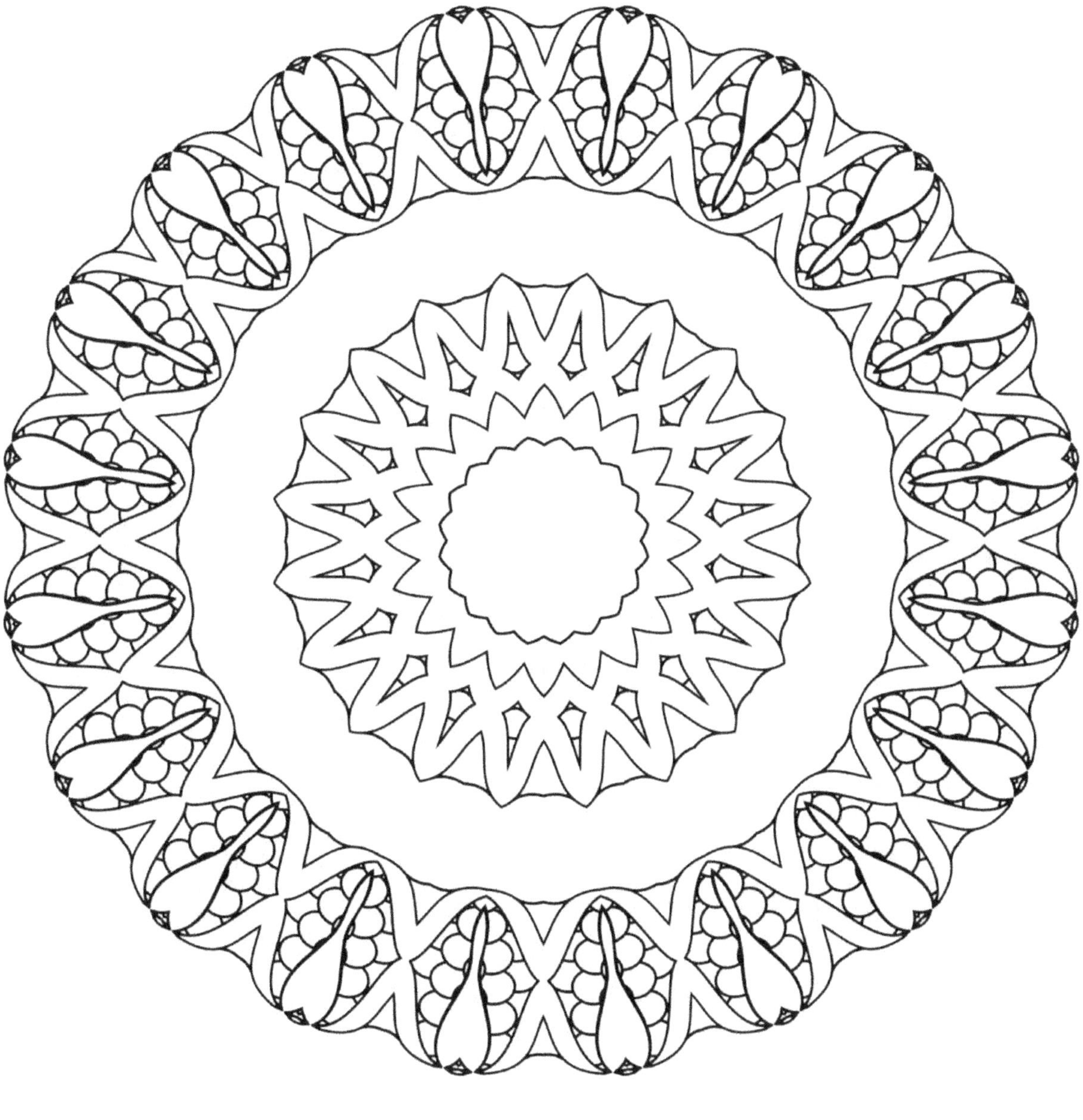

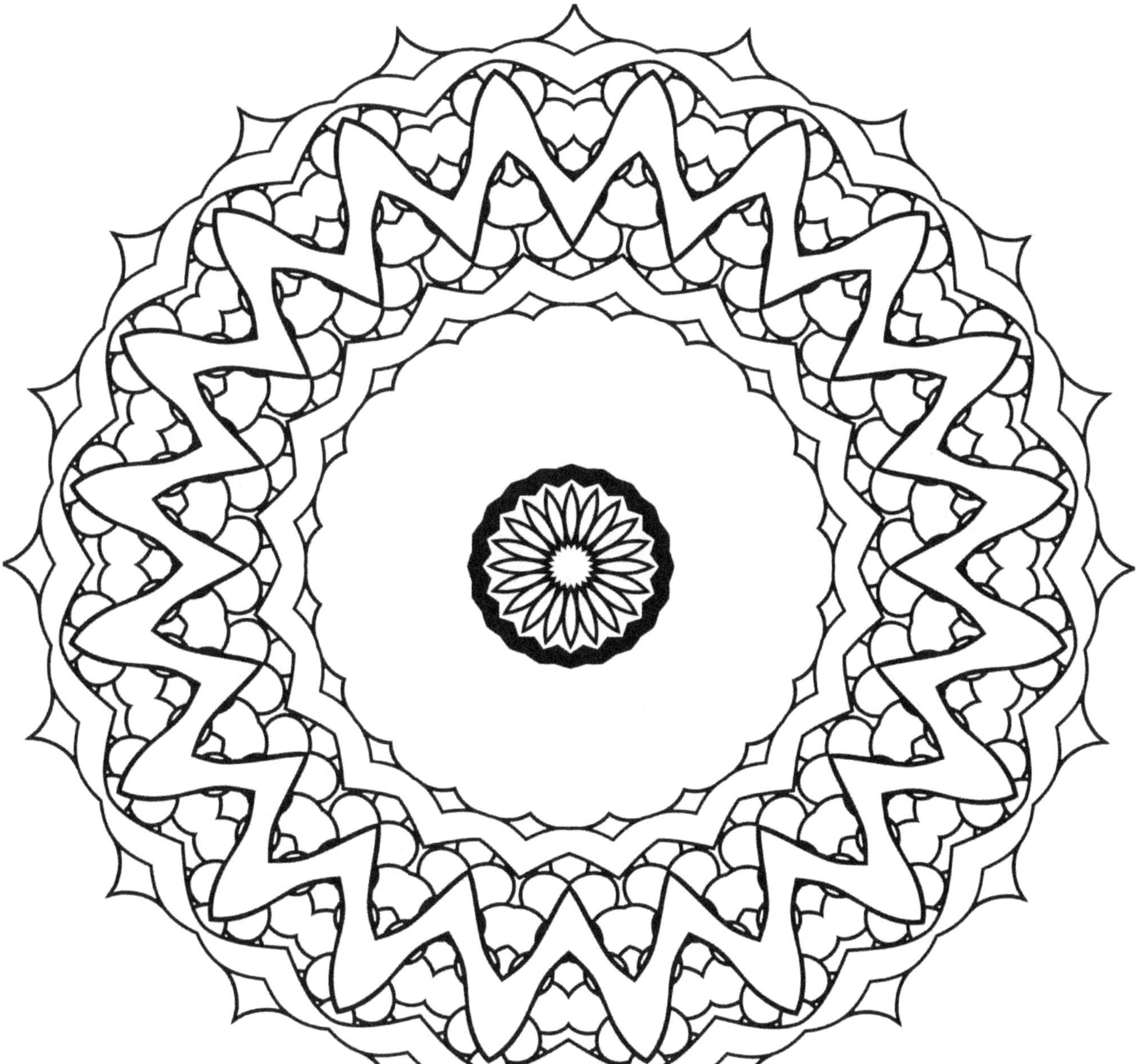

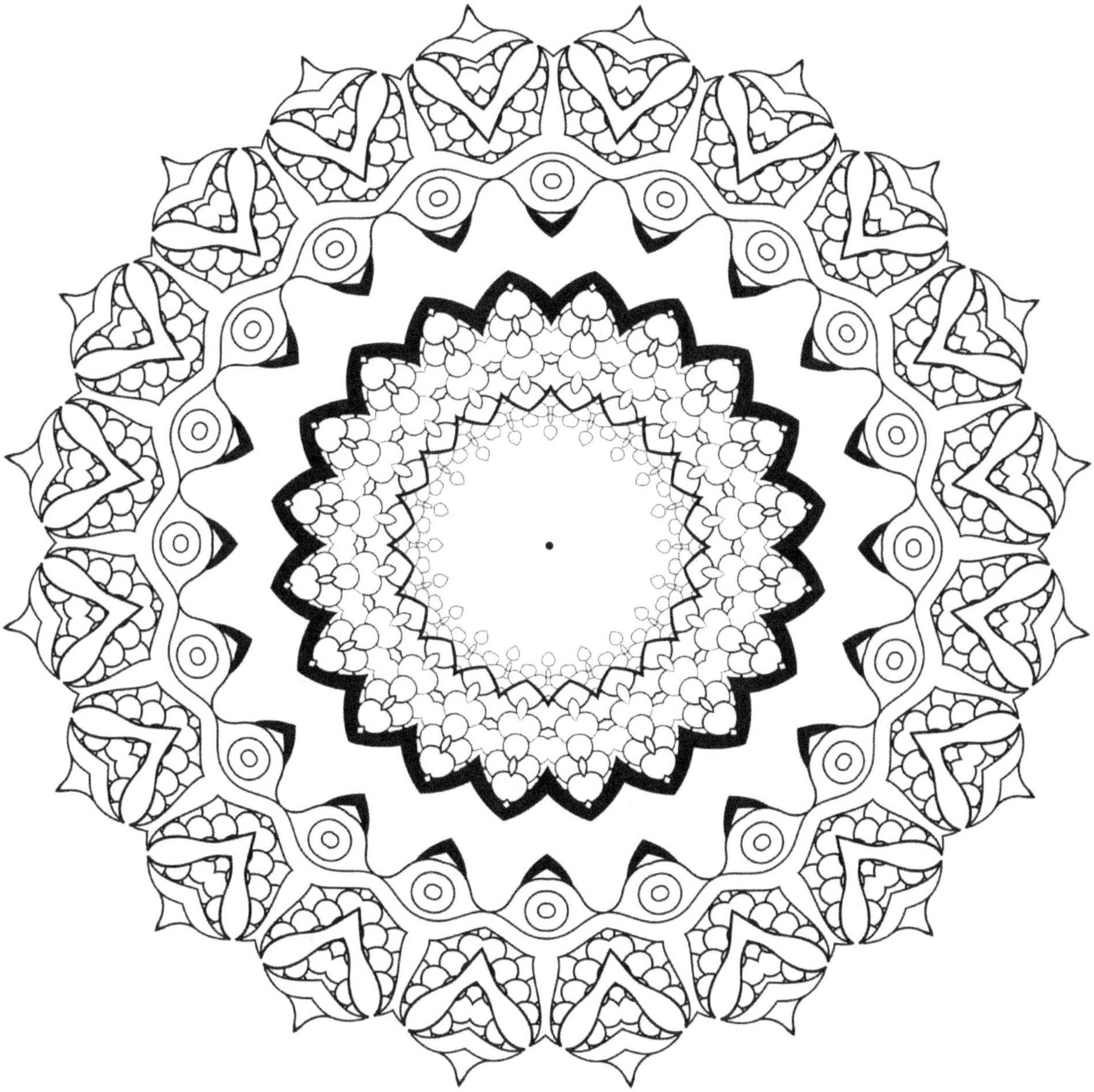

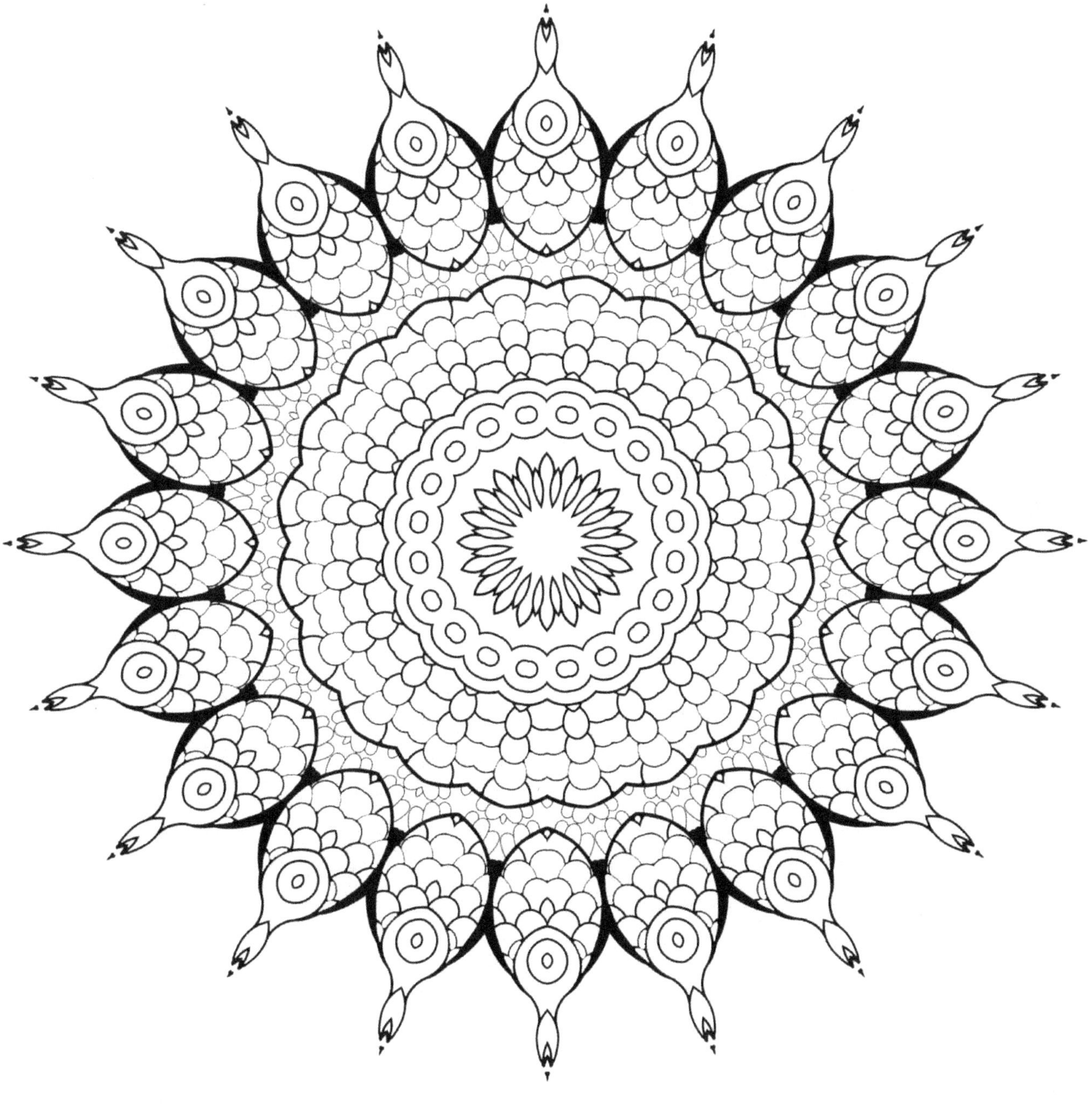

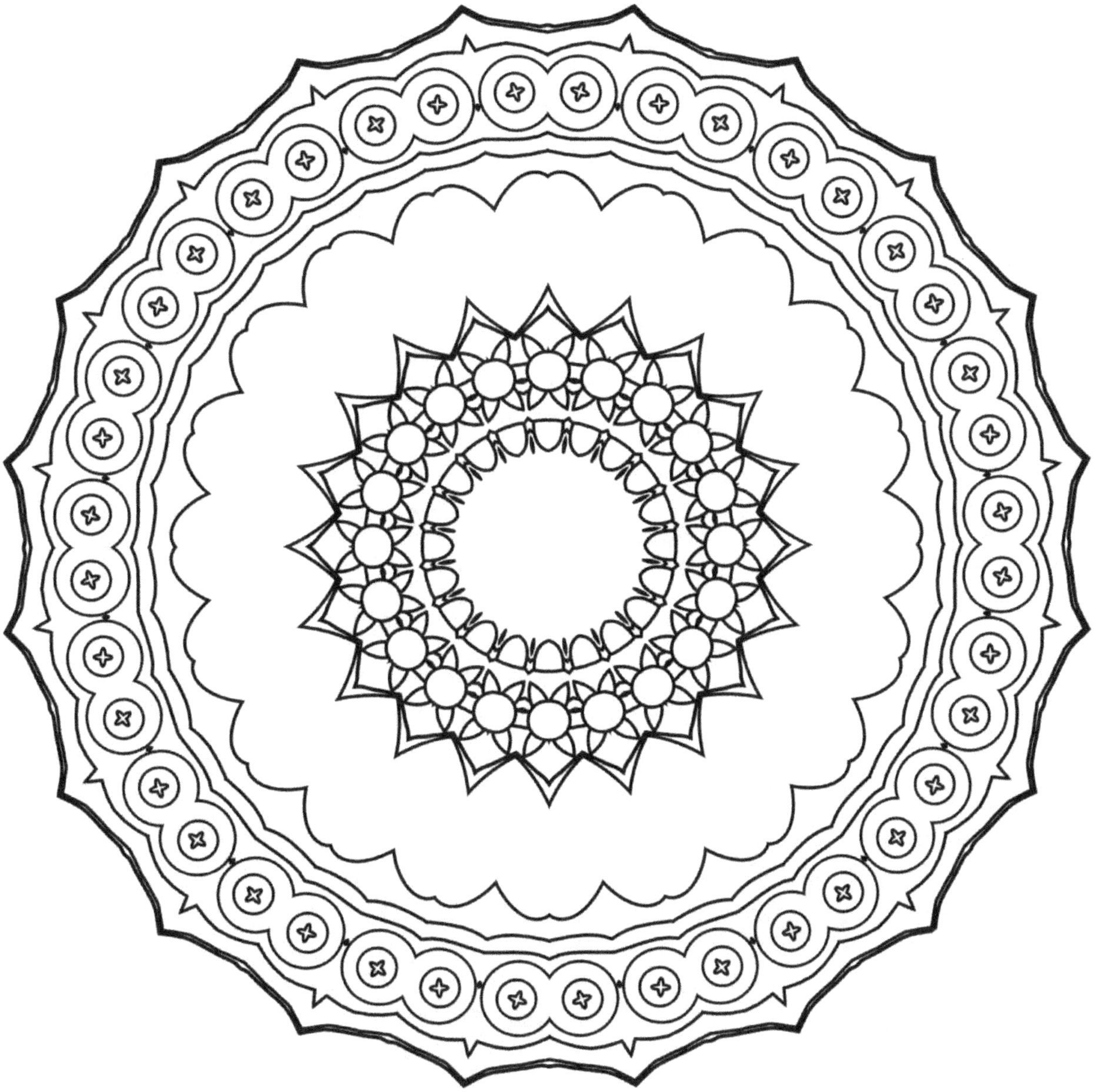

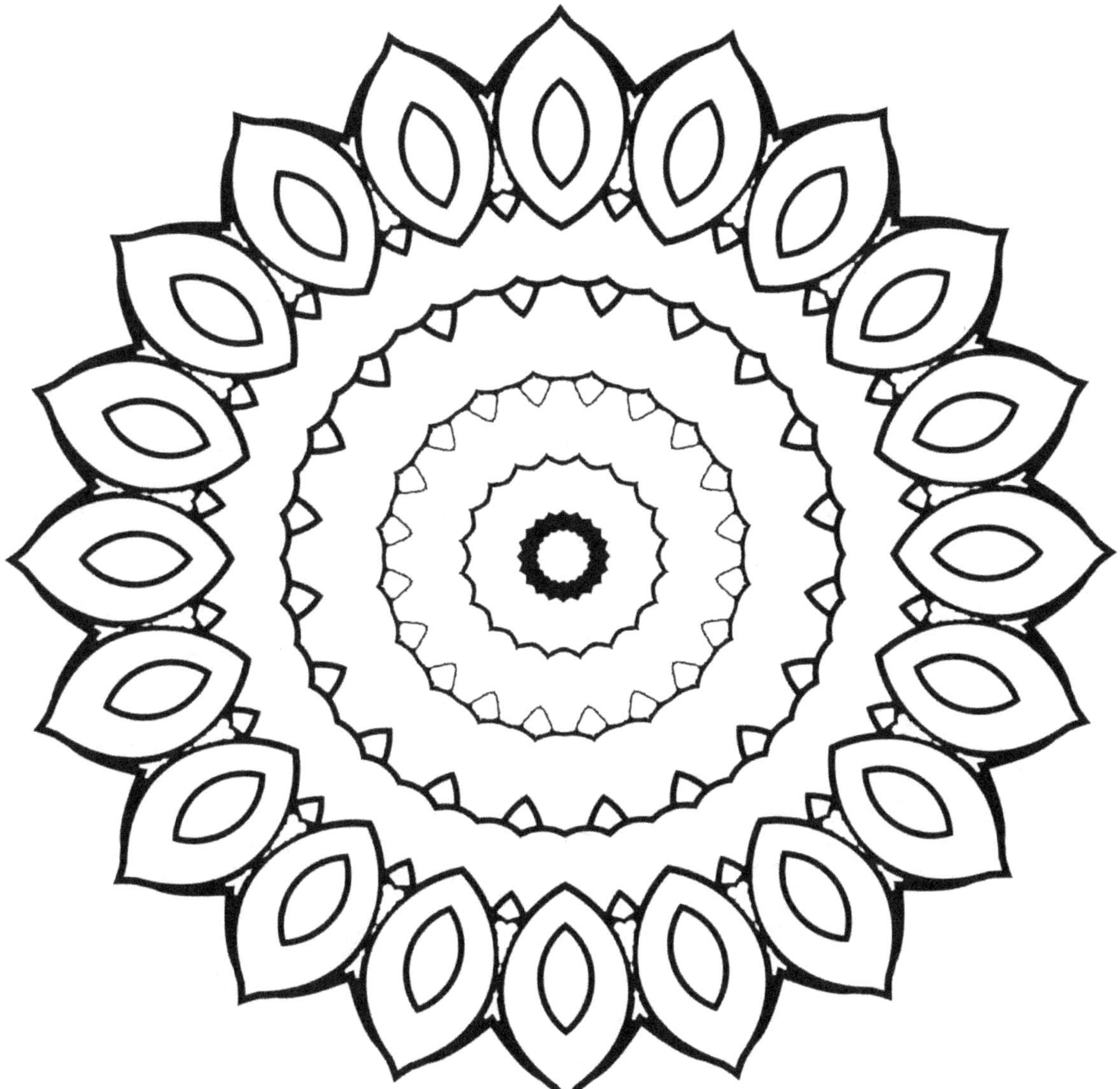

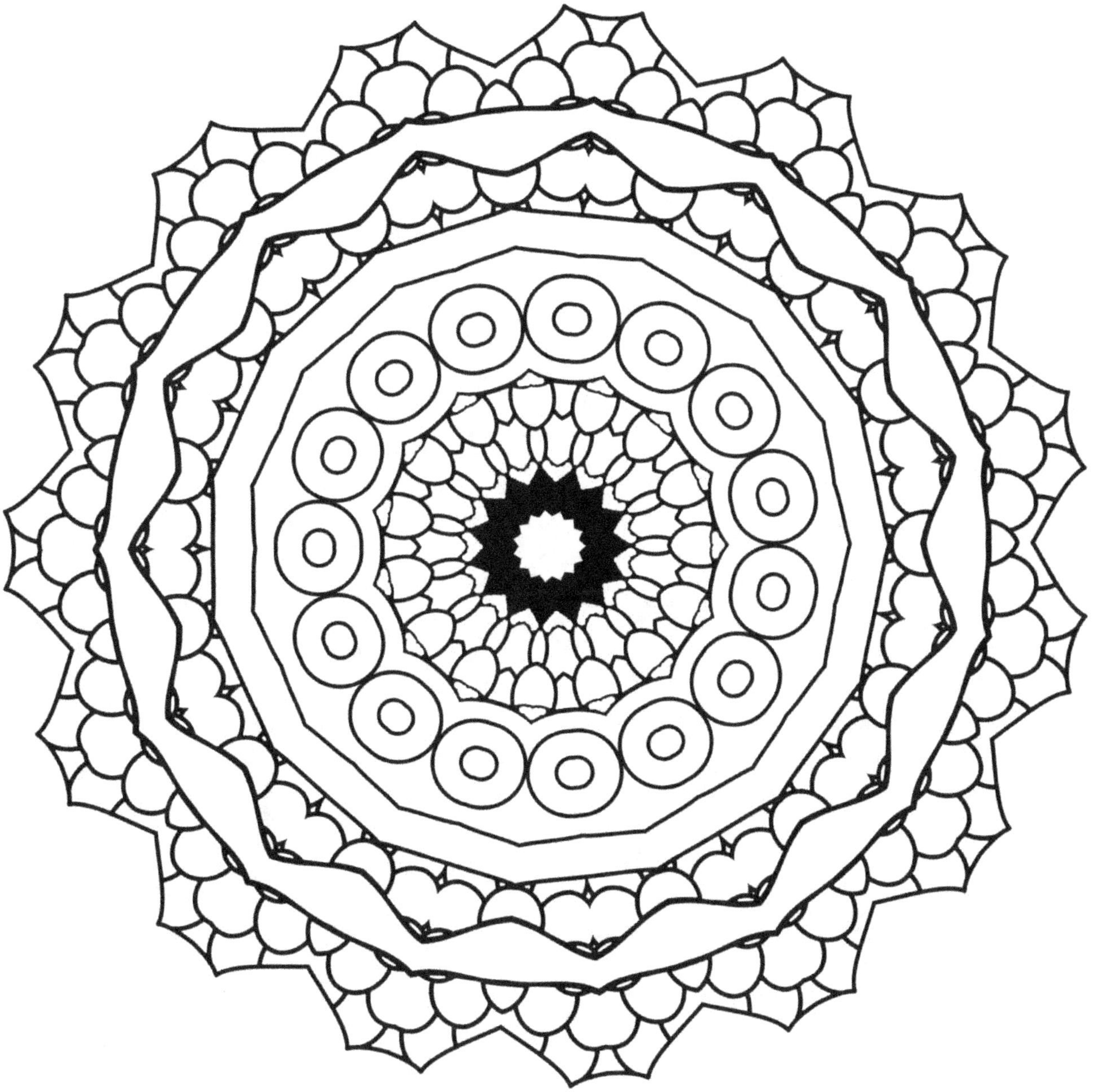

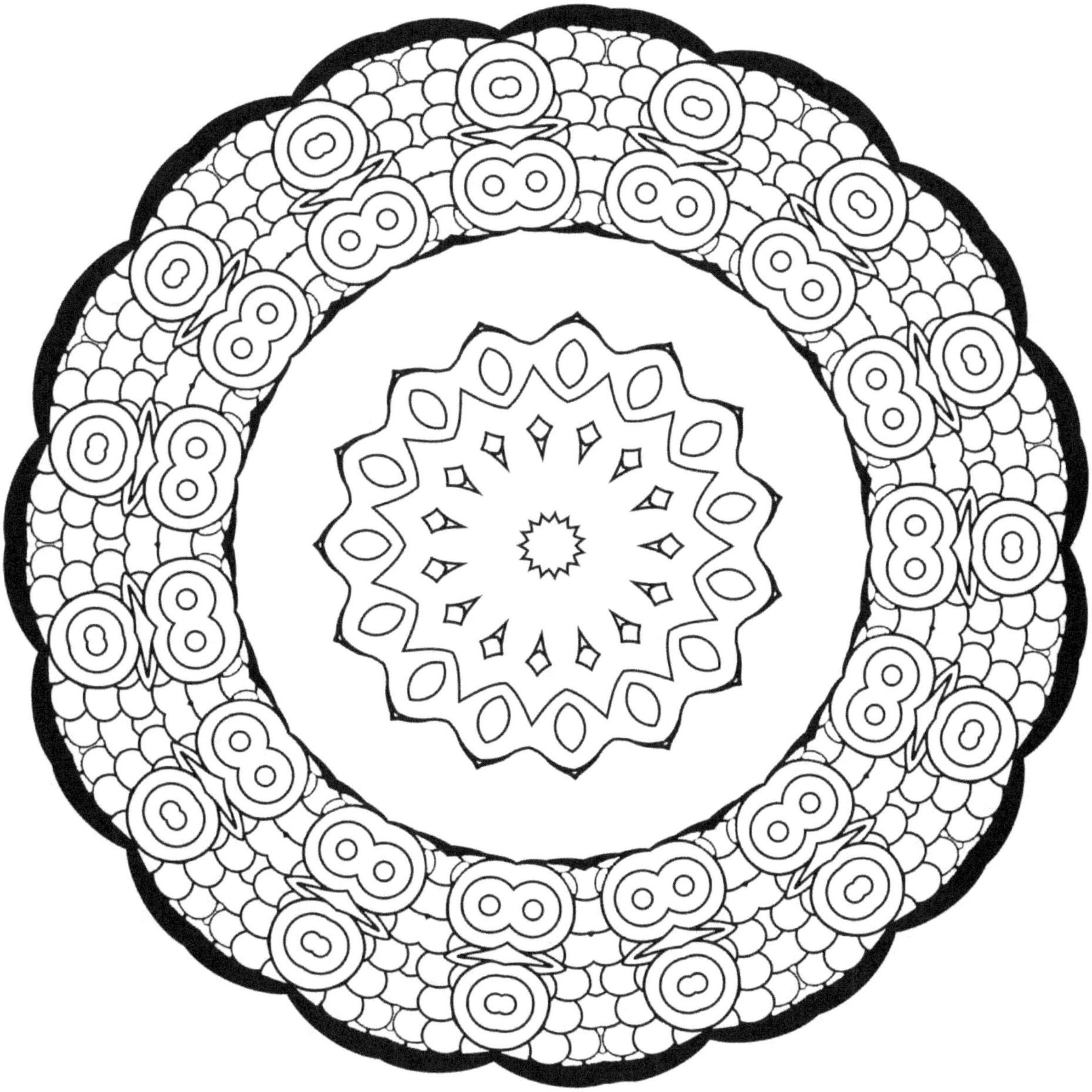

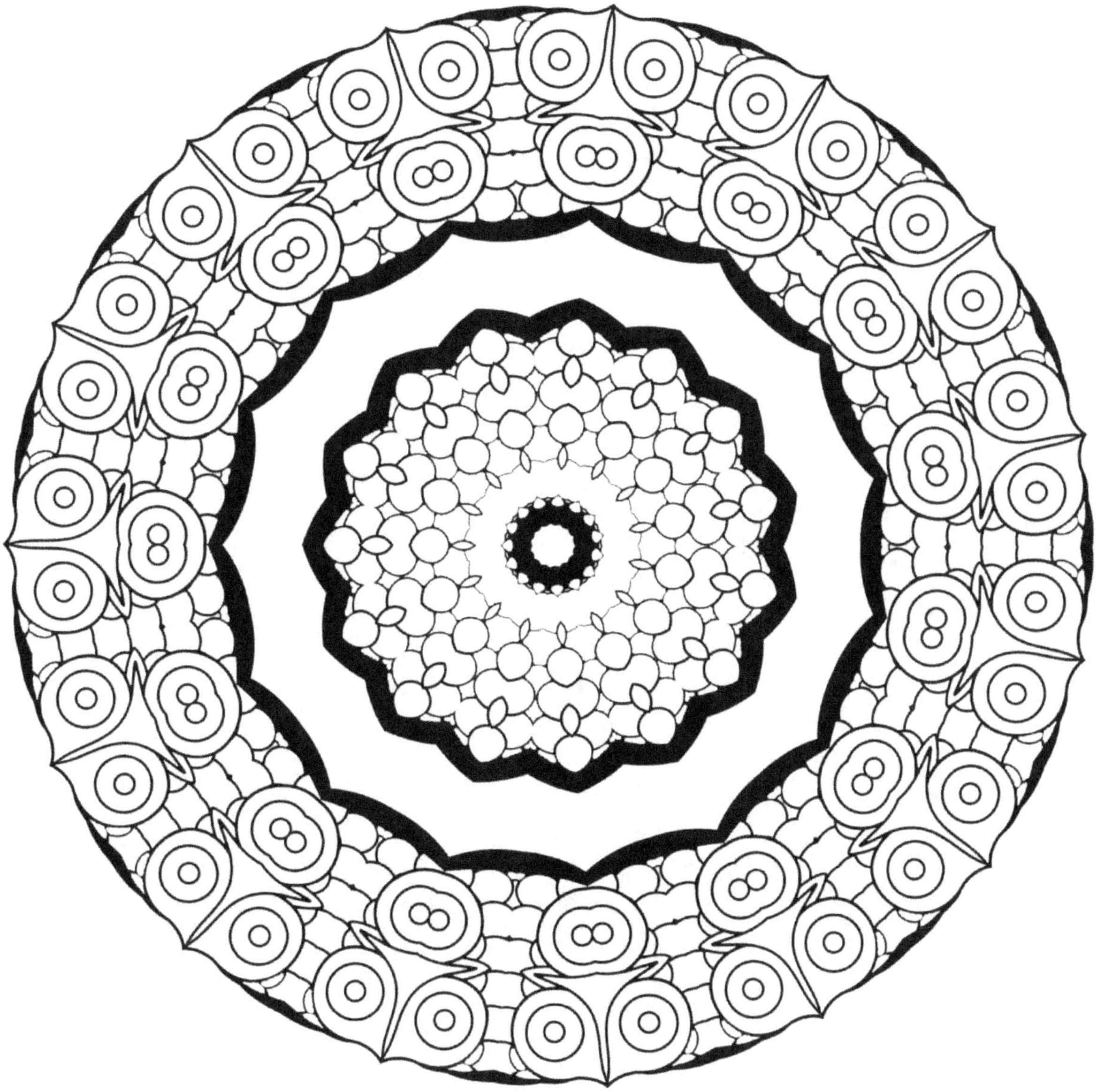

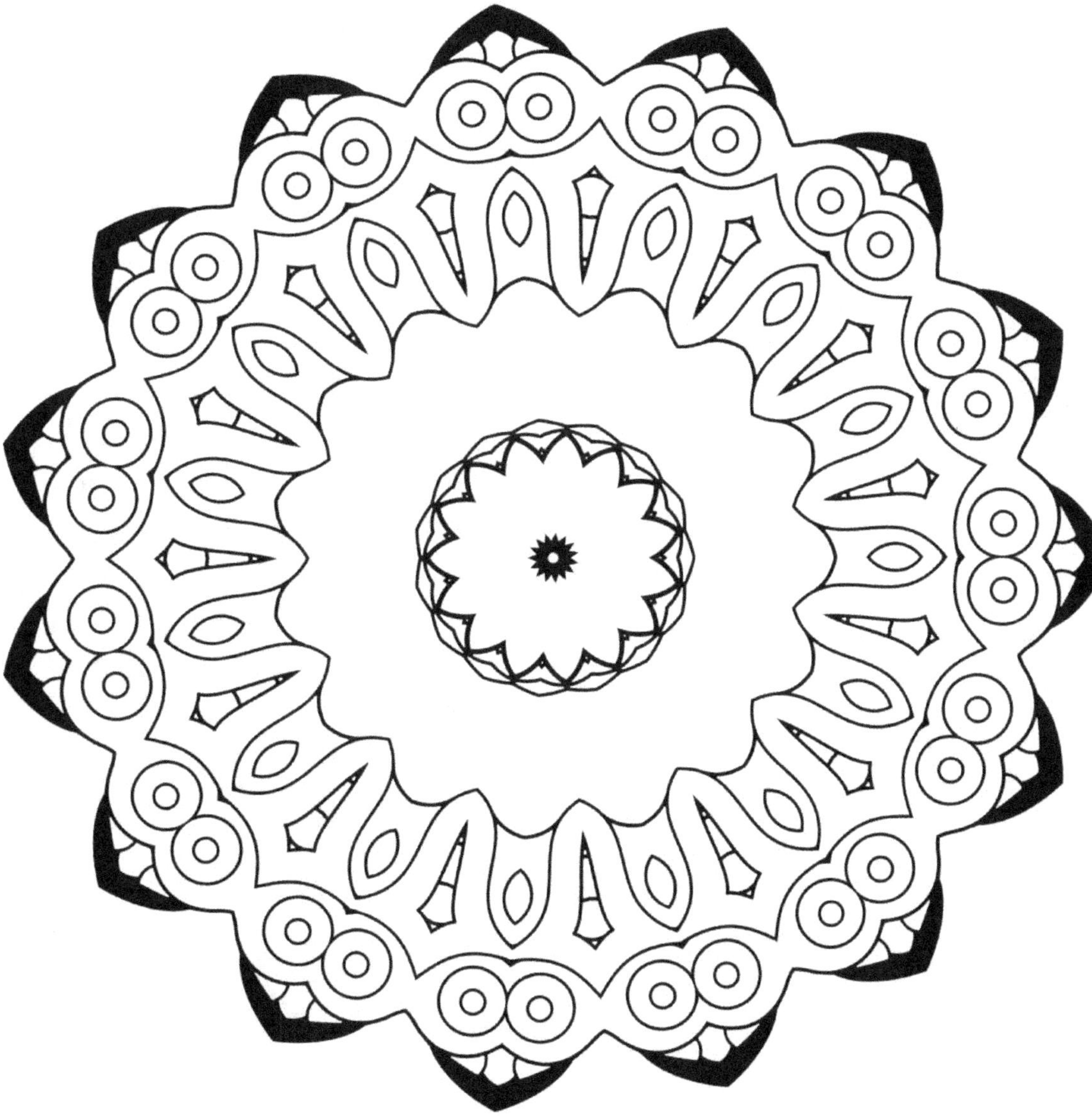

Thank you

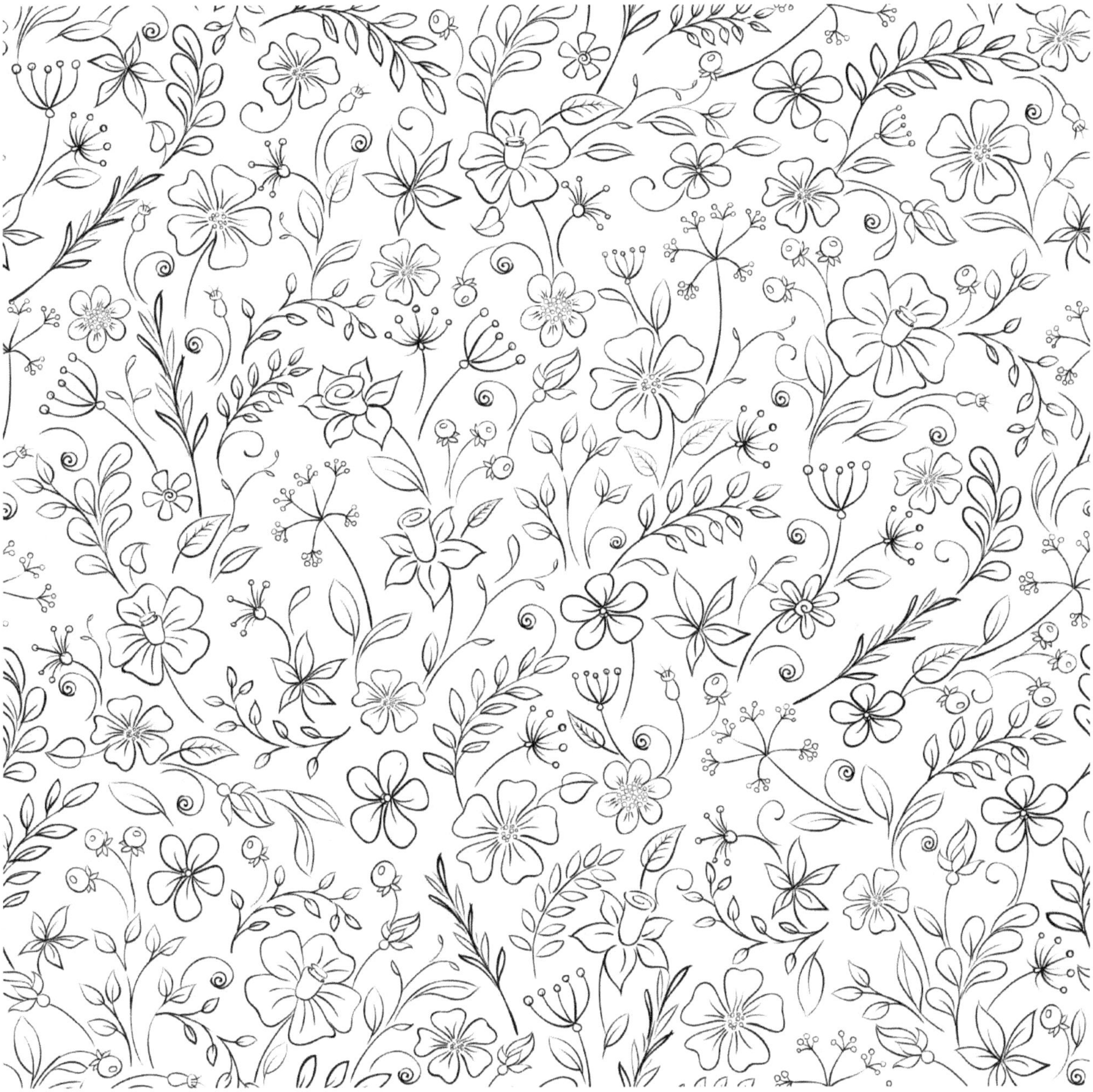

www.ingramcontent.com/pod-product-compliance
Lightning Source LLC
Chambersburg PA
CBHW081313170526
45166CB00011B/3516
* 9 7 8 1 5 1 9 5 9 6 3 1 4 *